Written by Sean Callery and Geraint Thomas

Contents

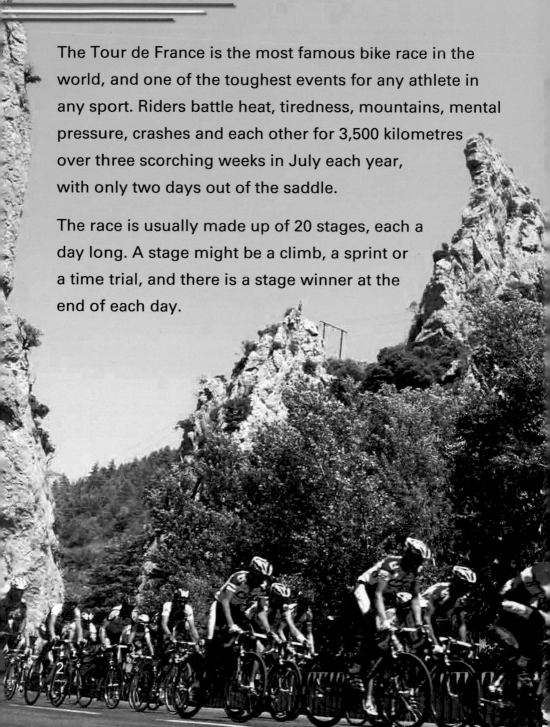

Introduction

The Tour de France is the most famous bike race in the world, and one of the toughest events for any athlete in any sport. Riders battle heat, tiredness, mountains, mental pressure, crashes and each other for 3,500 kilometres over three scorching weeks in July each year, with only two days out of the saddle.

The race is usually made up of 20 stages, each a day long. A stage might be a climb, a sprint or a time trial, and there is a stage winner at the end of each day.

It's a team race with an individual winner. Teams work together and use the strengths of individual members at each stage to help each other and ensure the overall time of all their members is quicker than the other teams. However, only the fastest individual winner is named at the end. The overall winner after three weeks of racing is the rider with the shortest time – he might not have won a single stage, but he will be the most **consistent** rider.

At the start there are between 20 and 22 teams of nine cyclists, but a fifth of those 200 riders won't cross the final finish line in Paris. Some will stop because their job of helping the team is done before then. Others will be too worn out to carry on.

Riders and teams from around the world are invited to compete and every professional cyclist dreams of taking part in the Tour de France. It can be dangerous and uncomfortable: bikes have ended up in the branches of trees, and one year some stuck to the road because it was so hot that the tar had melted!

The Tour de France is a national spectacle in France, where it's part of the nation's culture. The French respect the bravery and **endurance** that the race rewards, and enjoy the fact that it takes the cyclists around the sunflower fields and green vineyards of the French countryside.

Every day during the Tour de France, crowds of tens of thousands turn out to watch the cyclists zoom past from the roadside. Many more watch the race on TV – the only events with a higher total worldwide audience are the Olympics and the football World Cup.

Beginnings

The Tour de France was created to sell newspapers, or rather, one newspaper.

At the beginning of the 20th century, cycling was a big sport in France and was covered by the main sports paper, *Le Vélo*, which sold 80,000 copies a day. In the days before television and radio, people found out what was happening from newspapers.

In 1900 a **rival** paper started up. Initially this paper was called *L'Auto-Vélo*, but this later changed to *L'Auto*. The early days of *L'Auto* weren't very successful and the editor, Henri Desgrange, decided it needed a major **publicity** boost.

One of his reporters, Geo Lefevre, suggested a big cycling road race. There were already professional cyclists who earned their living by racing.

Henri Desgrange

a copy of *L'Auto* from 1903

But up until then, these popular races were either track circuits at a **velodrome** or shorter road races, and none lasted more than six days. Lefevre's suggestion was a massive five-week road race in six stages over 2,500 kilometres around France.

Desgrange loved the idea: readers would buy *L'Auto* to find out where and when the race was happening, then they'd buy it again the next day to find out who'd won that day's race. They'd have to keep buying the paper to find out how the race was going.

When the race was announced, though, its scale was so daunting that few riders entered. To gain more interest, Desgrange reduced the entry fee and shortened the timescale of the race to three weeks, but kept the distance the same. He increased the winner's prize from 12,000 to 20,000 **francs** – nearly ten times the annual wage of the average **manual worker** at the time.

It worked, and 60 cyclists were on the starting line of the first Tour de France on 1 July 1903. Only 21 made it to the finish line though.

the start of the Tour de France in 1903

the 1903 Tour de France

The race contained six long stages and competitors were expected to ride through the night on their heavy bicycles along bumpy roads that were little better than farm tracks. These surfaces were as hard as rock under the hot sun, but turned into muddy soup when it rained. The Tour de France was never meant to be easy!

Desgrange promoted the Tour de France as a tough endurance test and wrote about the riders as superheroes:

"The men waved their hats, the ladies their umbrellas. One felt they would have liked to touch the steel muscles of the most courageous champions since **antiquity**. *Who will carry off the first prize, entering the* **pantheon** *where only supermen may go?"*

9

Maurice Garin with his bike

The winner of the first Tour de France was Maurice Garin, who finished two hours and 47 minutes ahead of his nearest rival at 94 hours, 33 minutes and 14 seconds.

By the second Tour de France in 1904 some riders had devised ways of giving themselves an unfair advantage. A few cyclists were seen hitching lifts from cars, while others caught trains to get ahead. There was even a story of one competitor cycling with a cork in his mouth, attached to a length of wire and tied to a car which was pulling him along! Because the race continued through the night and over very long distances, it was difficult to monitor such behaviour.

spectators putting stones on the road to disrupt the race in 1904

The spectators also behaved badly. They beat up rivals of their heroes, threw stones, and scattered nails and broken glass in front of them to cause punctures. Cars drove alongside riders and tried to force them into ditches. Trees were even felled and laid across the road to block the route.

The 1904 winner was declared to be Henri Cornet, who actually crossed the line in fifth place. Garin had finished first, but was disqualified along with many others.

Henri Cornet

11

Desgrange claimed to be furious at the cheating and threatened not to run the event again. But his outrage was probably just for publicity. Instead, the 1905 Tour was ridden in daytime only, and the riders had to follow very strict rules. For example, riders who accepted any help got a time penalty. They also had to finish with the same clothes they started in – so they couldn't get someone else to carry their wool jackets in the heat of the day.

Louis Trousselier wins the 1905 Tour de France.

Over the following century the Tour de France became a team race and many of the rules were altered, such as making all cyclists wear helmets, but it remains a test of cycling endurance over three weeks. *L'Auto* later changed its name to *L'Équipe*, and is still popular today.

With the help of the Tour de France it had already defeated its rival *Le Vélo*, which closed in 1904.

No help allowed

In 1913, Eugène Christophe was hurtling down a mountain when the forks on his bike broke. Riders were not allowed to have any help in the race, so he jogged ten kilometres down the mountain and carried his broken bike to the local blacksmith. He heated a metal tube and hammered it to join the broken parts back together. After three hours of hot toil, the bike was fixed. But although he had mended his bike himself, a boy at the blacksmith's had assisted him and Christophe was given a ten-minute time penalty anyway.

Geraint Thomas

I'm Geraint Thomas and I'm a professional cyclist with Team Sky. I've won lots of track cycling **titles**, plus a team gold in the 2008 Olympics. Whenever people find out I'm a cyclist they always ask me about the Tour de France. I ride road and track races all around the world, and I can tell you that this is the biggest bike race on the planet!

I was born in Cardiff, South Wales, in 1986. When I was ten I went swimming at my local leisure centre and saw an advertisement for the Maindy Flyers, the local cycling club, so I went along to try it.

I competed from the very start, and loved it. We went training every Thursday and did races against each other every Tuesday. At first there were only five or six of us, but when I was 12 or 13 there were a lot more kids to race against. There was one boy who always used to beat me, but I practised really hard and eventually managed to become the best in the team. There was a good gang of us who'd travel all over the UK, taking on other riders.

We'd travel to the races in a minibus, camp overnight, have a barbeque and then the next day we'd race. It was great fun! We never took it too seriously, but looking back it was then that I learnt all the racing and riding skills I have today.

I won lots of junior titles and turned professional in 2007. That was when I completed my first Tour de France. At 21 I was the youngest rider that year.

I'd dreamt about racing in the Tour de France since I was a kid. I'd run home from school and watch coverage of the race on the television, and at the end of the programme they'd show the top riders. I used to imagine my name on that list.

Taking part in the Tour de France is an amazing experience, but riding in it for the first time was the hardest thing I'd done by far. I've never suffered as much as I did in those three weeks. Every night I thought, "I can't go through that again tomorrow." But as soon as I got on my bike the next day I'd say to myself, "Come on, just finish today" – because it was the Tour de France.

my first Tour de France in 2007

Equipment

If a competitor from the first Tour de France time-travelled to today's race, he'd probably recognise the bikes but think the riders were from outer space.

Early riders wore caps, woollen jackets, long trousers and goggles to protect their eyes from dusty roads. Their protection from the hot sun was a cooling cabbage leaf under their caps! Riders also rested a piece of steak on their saddles to soften the impact of the rough roads.

Nowadays cycling shorts are padded for comfort, and racing cyclists wear figure-hugging gear that reduces air resistance and allows their skin to breathe, so that they don't get covered in sweat. They have wraparound shades and streamlined helmets. Racing cyclists wear special shoes made of lightweight material that lock on to the pedals, allowing the rider to pull as well as push the pedals round.

The bikes may look similar to the ones that were used in 1903, but they've changed technically and in their use of materials.

Competitors in the early races rode heavy steel-framed bikes. They had to be strong to cope with hours of pounding along uneven roads.

Modern bike frames are made from light, strong materials such as carbon fibre or titanium. The Tour de France rules say racing bikes must weigh no less than 6.8 kilograms. Sometimes they are so light that mechanics have to add fittings just before a race to get the weight up to the minimum.

Early bikes had two fixed gears, one on each side of the back wheel. To climb a hill, riders switched this back wheel round to use the lower gear. When they wanted more speed, they had to get off and fit it round the other way.

But from 1937 Tour riders were allowed to use derailleur gears. These move the chain to a different **sprocket** so that the back wheel turns fewer or more times on the same number of pedal **revolutions**. Today, cyclists can choose from about 20 gears at the flick of a switch.

Every rider has to force their way through the air, battling against wind resistance. Racing bikes are tested in wind tunnels to find ways to reduce this drag. For instance the wheels might only have three **spokes** to help the bike slice through the air.

testing a bike in a wind tunnel

Professional cyclists have computers on their bikes
that tell them their average speed and how far they've
travelled. They also have two-way radios so that they can
talk with the team manager during the race.

Set the bar low

To ride fast, riders set the handlebars
low so that they can lean into
the wind. On the final day of the
1989 competition, Greg LeMond took
this a step further with a pair of
handlebars stretched forwards so
that he could rest his elbows on them
and tuck his body in like a skier,
with his nose just over the spinning
front wheel.

LeMond ignored the stares of baffled
spectators and sped along at an average of 54.5 kilometres
per hour to beat his rival by eight seconds, the narrowest ever
margin of victory across the whole Tour. The new handlebars
won the title for him. These aerobars, also called tribars,
are now standard equipment on time trials.

Geraint Thomas

I have a race bike, a spare race bike and a training bike. Each of these is set up exactly the same, down to the last millimetre. This is to prevent injuries, because if our position is even slightly different from one bike to another we won't be used to it and could end up having an accident. The training bike stays at home, but the race bike and spare bike go everywhere with me. We push them so hard across so many kilometres and there are often crashes, so I usually get through about four bikes a year!

on my race bike

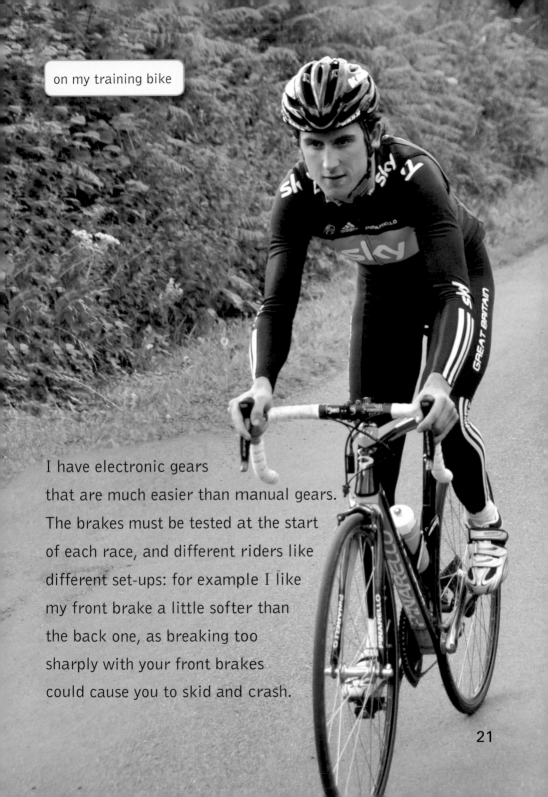

on my training bike

I have electronic gears
that are much easier than manual gears.
The brakes must be tested at the start
of each race, and different riders like
different set-ups: for example I like
my front brake a little softer than
the back one, as breaking too
sharply with your front brakes
could cause you to skid and crash.

The Tour de France today

It's traditional for French people to take their annual holiday in July, and the three-week Tour de France race has become part of that holiday. They catch up with the latest news online, on TV, radio and in the newspapers. Two billion people around the world watch with them.

The route changes every year, although it always takes riders on a circuit, switching each year between a clockwise and anti-clockwise direction. However, because each stage doesn't always start where the previous one finished, sometimes the whole Tour de France operation travels to a new starting point for the next day.

The Badger

An ex-Tour de France rider called Bernard Hinault helps to decide the route each year. He was a successful rider who won the Tour de France five times between 1978 and 1985, earning himself the nickname "The Badger" because, like that very tough animal, he 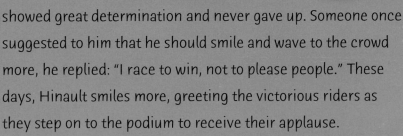 showed great determination and never gave up. Someone once suggested to him that he should smile and wave to the crowd more, he replied: "I race to win, not to please people." These days, Hinault smiles more, greeting the victorious riders as they step on to the podium to receive their applause.

Since 1954 some stages have been held in nearby countries. The Tour de France riders have cycled across parts of Belgium, Germany, Italy, Luxembourg, the Netherlands, Spain and Switzerland. They've even crossed the Channel to pedal through Ireland and Great Britain.

Portsmouth, Great Britain, 1994

the Netherlands, 2010

Towns are so keen to host a stage
start or finish in the Tour de France
that they pay the organisers to
be involved. This is partly because it
is an honour to be part of the Tour de
France, but they also do this because
of the publicity it will generate:
thousands of spectators visit and
the town is named in all the media
coverage of the event. Some towns
think it puts them "on the map".

Switzerland, 2009

Map of the Tour de France, 2010

25th July

France

This map shows the route that was used in the Tour de France in 2010. It shows the start and finish points for different stages through the three weeks of the race. Although every Tour de France has a different route, they all follow a similar pattern.

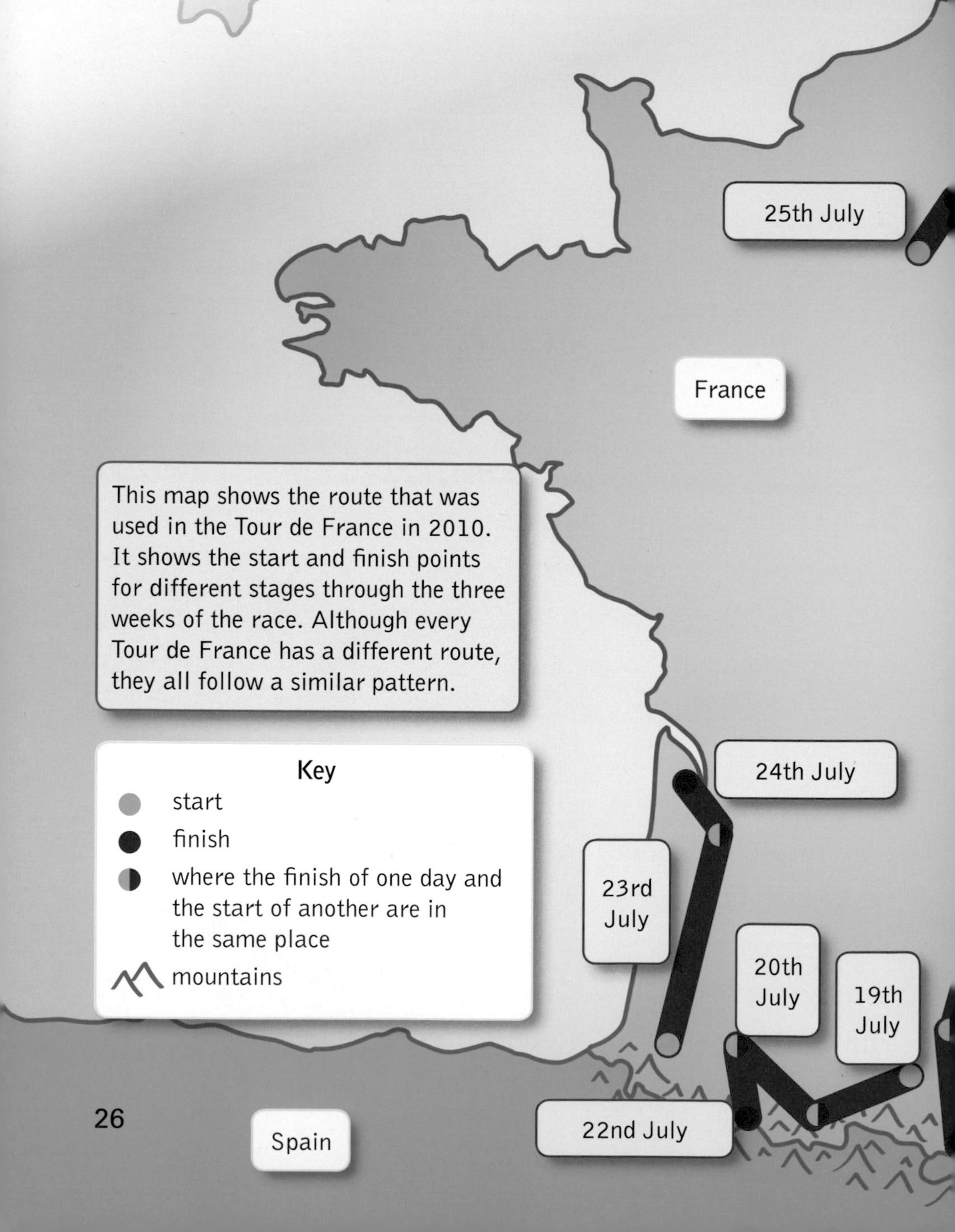

Key

- start
- finish
- where the finish of one day and the start of another are in the same place
- mountains

24th July

23rd July

20th July

19th July

22nd July

Spain

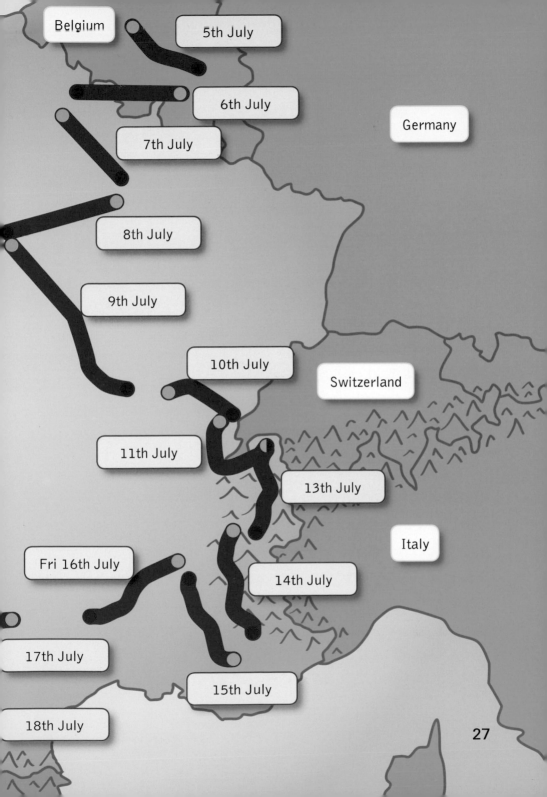

Belgium

5th July

6th July

Germany

7th July

8th July

9th July

10th July

Switzerland

11th July

13th July

Italy

Fri 16th July

14th July

17th July

15th July

18th July

27

the four winning jerseys

The stages vary between climbing, **sprinting** or
time trialling, and various prizes are awarded at
the end of the entire race. The best climber is called
the "King of the Mountains" and wins a white jersey with
red dots. The fastest sprinter wins a green jersey and
the best young rider under the age of 26 gets a white
jersey. There's also a team prize based on the scores of
the first three finishers in each team. The most glory goes
to the overall winner, the rider with the shortest time in
the whole 21-day event, who wins a yellow jersey.

The yellow jersey is the most famous top in cycling. It is awarded each day to the race leader, to be worn on the following stage, as well as to the overall winner at the end of the race. The tradition began in 1919 so that spectators and officials could easily pick out the top rider. Some believe that its colour was chosen because the newspaper sponsor, *L'Auto*, was printed on yellow paper. Another story goes that the sports shop only had enough stock of that colour. Either way, **le maillot jaune** marks its wearer out as the target everyone wants to beat.

Geraint Thomas

My second Tour de France was in 2010. I'd just won
the National Championships and knew I was on good form,
but didn't have any expectations for this race. I was just there
to help my team, and had no personal ambitions – I didn't
think I'd have the chance to do well! Overall the team didn't
do as well that year as we'd hoped, so although we learnt
a lot, we were all feeling a bit disappointed. Then I was
awarded the best young rider and won the white jersey
between stages three and five. It was so unexpected. It was
the highlight of the race for me and for the team.

When I was a kid I used to watch the winners on the podium
and dreamt of one day being there – I never thought it would be
a reality. Jersey wearers line up at the front of the peloton,
and that made me feel extra special. It gave me the confidence
to show everyone that I could win stages in the future, and
possibly even get the yellow jersey.
It would be a proud feeling to
represent British cycling by wearing
the yellow jersey, so it's still a big
goal of mine.

Tour de France, 2010

The people

There can be 30 riders in a professional cycling team. They compete throughout the year in races around the world, but only nine riders win the honour of cycling for their team in the Tour de France. The nine cyclists need a range of skills to ensure there is a strong contender in each stage of the race, e.g. a good climber, a fast rider for sprints etc. A lead rider, the best overall cyclist in the team, is chosen by the team manager, based on their success over the course of the year. The cyclists are not the only people involved in the race, though. Behind the scenes, thousands of people help to run the Tour de France.

The teams have sports coaches who organise training and preparation for the race. They are led by a team manager who makes key decisions about how the team is run, who will race and how. Looking after the riders' bodies are the masseurs who help to keep their muscles working. Looking after the bikes are the mechanics, known as "wrenches".

a wrench

Wrench work

The wrenches set up each bike so that it's just right for its rider and that day's race. They are also on hand to deal with punctures and mechanical faults. Sometimes they have to work on the move – literally. The team car pulls up alongside the rider whose bike has a problem and he leans out of the window, tools in hand, and fixes it. If it's a puncture, the rider stops and the wrenches whip off the wheel and clip in a new one in just a few seconds. In the evening, while the riders relax, the mechanics repair and clean the bikes for the next day.

Around 70 people are employed to work on arrangements and planning for the race all year round. During the actual event, about 220 extra staff are hired to help with **implementing** these plans, which include supplying refreshments to the cyclists and monitoring safety. Another 500 people are also brought in to do the heavy work such as moving barriers, putting up stages and signposting the route. All these jobs are crucial to ensure that the race runs smoothly and any problems are sorted out quickly.

The soigneurs – from the French word meaning "to care for", have to book the hotels, check the washing gets done, buy and prepare food and do any other jobs that are necessary. Finally there are the drivers of the team bus and other vehicles. They have to drive along difficult roads without harming their precious cargo – the riders and the equipment for each race.

It takes a lot of money to keep this business running. Firms from outside the world of cycling pay large amounts of money in return for having a team named after them and displaying their logo. These sponsors want to put their name in front of millions of people who watch the Tour de France.

Two French TV stations film the Tour de France during the race. They have a staff of about 300 people, and equipment including four helicopters, two light aircraft, two motorcycles and many other trucks and cars. There are also radio staff for more than 70 stations, 450 print and online journalists and around 240 photographers.

To capture every moment of the Tour on film, cameramen have to keep up – usually helped by a motorbike.

Getting ready

Tour de France riders are professional athletes. They cycle 32,000–40,000 kilometres in races and training every year. That's twice the distance the average car is driven, and it's all powered by their bodies, so they have to be very fit.

Preparation for the Tour starts with base training. This is cycling for about six hours a day outside, at a steady pace, to build basic fitness. After a month or two, the riders pedal harder in bursts for shorter distances. This could be an hour-long trawl at a high rate of pedalling, or a minute sprint on full power.

Throughout this training the team coaches will measure their cyclists' heart rates and the amount of oxygen they are getting into their bodies to check that they aren't pushing themselves too hard.

As part of their preparation for the tour, cyclists enter smaller races throughout the year. Before each race starts, riders work up a sweat by cycling on the road or on rollers, which allow the cyclist to practise speed and balance without moving forward. This gets blood flowing into their muscles to make them warm. Muscles are like a length of elastic and cold muscles are more likely to snap.

These muscles would stop working properly if the cyclists stopped riding on their rest days. Instead, they keep their legs moving with smooth, relaxing rides.

training on rollers

Professional cyclists protect their skin, too. This means more than smearing on sun cream, they also shave their legs. This is because they get saddle sores and cuts, which are much easier to treat when the skin is smooth and without hair.

Seven times better

American cyclist Lance Armstrong is one of the legends of the Tour de France because he won it seven times in a row between 1999 and 2005. He kept his body in tip-top condition after recovering from cancer in the 1990s. He also trained himself to pedal at a higher cadence. Cadence is the rate at which cyclists turn their pedals, measured in revolutions per minute (rpm). While his competitors aimed for a cadence of 90 rpm, rising to 120 rpm in sprints, Armstrong pushed himself to 110 rpm and kept going at this higher rate for hours at a time, staying down in the saddle rather than standing to push the pedals harder, which would have tired him out sooner. He also took preparation for the Tour de France to a new level, riding parts of the course in advance so that he knew the route and any problems he might encounter on it.

Geraint Thomas

In a road race I average around 75 rpm for six hours and can ride uphill for two to three hours. For this, a lot of strength and endurance is needed: that's why I train.

I love to get out on my bike. Most of the time I don't see it as training, it's just a hobby I love. In fact, I don't feel right if I don't get on my bike every day — I even go for a ride on Christmas Day! If I've been travelling I go for a ride when I arrive at my destination. It's good for your legs after sitting still in an aeroplane or on a coach.

During training, I will often have a few "efforts". They range from 20-second sprints to long 30-minute hill climbs.

training on my bike in Wales

40

training at the velodrome

All my training is planned with my coach six months ahead of my big target. Obviously it changes on a day-to-day basis, but the general outline and goal for the week are decided months in advance. I don't do all my training out on the road. Sometimes I will ride on the rollers, or I go to the velodrome in Manchester for a training session. British cycling is based in Manchester, and I moved there when I was 18 so I could train with my team. I go to the velodrome between two and four times a week, and even cycle to get there. The sessions can be pretty hard going and it takes a lot out of you, but that makes the easy days even more enjoyable!

Food and drink

Racing takes a lot of energy out of the body, so the riders need plenty of fuel. The average person eats 2,000–3,000 calories a day. Professional cyclists burn about 5,000 calories on each day of the Tour de France so they need twice as much energy-giving food. They follow a very healthy diet with lots of fresh fruit and vegetables and plenty of pasta, rice and potatoes. These starchy foods are high in carbohydrates, which give the body energy.

During races, riders boost their energy levels with special energy bars and packs of energy gels. They pick up feedbags from feeding stations along the way, grabbing the pack without stopping their bike and then eating on the move.

Riders lose a lot of water through sweating. To stay hydrated they drink lots of refreshing water with added sugar and minerals to give them an extra boost. The drink containers that fit on to their bikes are often **insulated** to keep the liquid cool. Each rider carries two half-litre water bottles and on hot days they'll get through both every hour, picking up replacements from the support team as they zoom along.

A day on the Tour de France

A day on the Tour de France starts before the sun rises and finishes in moonlight. For some spectators it begins a few days earlier – some of them set up tents way ahead along the route so that they are in a good place to see the action on the day.

At dawn, the support team puts up barriers to keep the crowd back and the riders safe. Meanwhile, the teams wake up early and the riders cram in a big breakfast to give them plenty of energy for the start of the day. They discuss the team plan – are they going to ride from the front, or take their time and watch the other teams? Then it's on to the team bus and down to the Village, the area where the organisers are set up and fans mill around hoping to get pictures and autographs of their heroes. Here, TV crews and journalists try to pick up information and stories from the riders and get an idea of what might happen later on.

The advertising caravan sets off with the official cars and police motorcycles ensuring the road is clear.

the advertising caravan

Look at me!

The advertising caravan is a 20-kilometre-long convoy of 160 trucks and vans carrying advertising. They drive slowly along the route with music blasting out, throwing out gifts such as badges, hats and samples of their products. This caravan has been a major part of the Tour de France since 1930. The race organisers needed more money to fund the race, so allowed advertisers to drive along the route for a fee. The crowds of spectators love it.

Then the riders swoop through.
For the first few kilometres,
they stay together as a group
in what is known as a
rolling start. Then the Tour
director waves a white flag
and they start to race for real.

If there's a breakaway, the first riders into a town along
the route might be a small group or even a lone cyclist.
More likely, the peloton arrives – the main group of riders
– passing by in seconds.

The support vehicles follow, then the team vans with spare
equipment and food, police motorcycles and organisers'
cars. At the back is the "broom wagon". Since 1910 this
has been the vehicle that picks up riders who can ride no
more, by tradition a broom is ceremoniously hung on the
back! Although nowadays those who drop out climb into
the team car.

Sometimes the race is shown on a big screen in the town.
On quieter parts of the route people come out of their
houses and perch their TV on a window sill so that they
can keep watching the race on the TV once the cyclists
have gone past.

After about six hours on the road, the cyclists approach the finish line. Unless someone made a breakaway earlier on, this is where they pump their legs even harder for the sprint finish.

The day isn't over for the exhausted riders. The winners have to go straight to the medical area for drug testing, to make sure that no one has cheated by taking substances to improve their performance. Cameras and microphones are thrust towards the riders, and many fans gather near the team buses, clutching pens and paper for autographs.

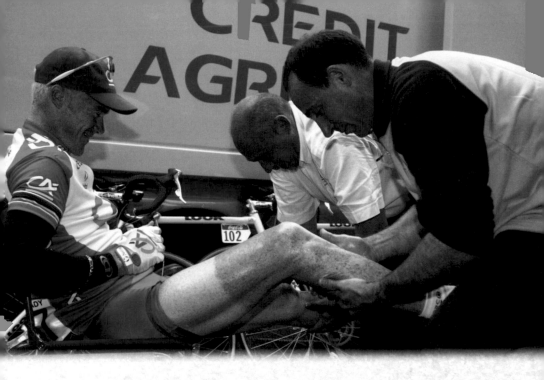

The day's winners climb on to the podium and take the
crowd's applause, then it's back on the bus and off to the
next hotel. Here they have a massage to ease the pain
in their tired muscles and keep them in good condition.
Many riders tweet or write blogs to keep in contact with
their fans. They are often away from their families, so they
may take some time to talk with them before easing their
aching legs into bed. The next day, it all happens again.

Meanwhile, the Tour support team dismantles the podium
and stacks the safety barriers on to trucks, ready to
assemble at the next day's location.

Geraint Thomas

I wake up three hours before the start of the day's race for breakfast, where I eat as much as possible, and talk! I talk about anything apart from the race that day. We do this to relax, because after three non-stop weeks of the Tour de France you could easily burn yourself out if you think about it too much in the mornings and evenings. We have a team meeting on the bus an hour before the start of the day's race to discuss the race, but that's it.

In the 2010 Tour I was in the front group, aiming to win, and the crowd was unbelievable. The noise gives you goosebumps, especially when you hear them calling out your name. There are flags from all over the world, but I always notice the Welsh and British ones. They definitely give you that extra motivation to keep going, knowing you have the support from back home. In Stage Three we rode towards a town called Arenberg. The route was cobbled, and I enjoyed the new challenge of cycling on those roads.

You can see the camera operators on the motorbikes and hear the helicopters filming all the action, and it's great to be racing at the front and experiencing it all!

The peloton

The peloton comes from the French word for platoon, or group, and looks like a racing rainbow because so many teams in their different colours are part of it. They hurtle along inches from each other, tucking in behind the rider in front. This use of the **slipstream** is called "drafting", and is the same method that birds use when they form a V formation in the sky.

Drafting gives a massive advantage: it has been estimated that a bike racer uses 80% of his energy to get through the air, and only 20% moving his bike. Drafting reduces the air resistance and saves about a third of the energy needed to ride a bike. Teams protect each other, and especially their top rider, by allowing them to ride close behind and by moving alongside the rider to block any crosswind.

There was no peloton in the Tour de France until the 1930s, because the race organiser, Henri Desgrange, didn't like riders working together. Also, bikes in the 1930s went at very different speeds. It was the introduction of derailleur gears that allowed riders to stay together at the same pace and the peloton was born.

54

Some riders have special jobs in the peloton. The rouleurs are sprinters who chase after riders from other teams who try to break away ahead of the main group.
The "domestiques" help the team by picking up supplies and messages from the team car.

Unless it's a tough mountain climb – when the peloton tends to get stretched out into a line – riders often bunch together to chat to each other, sharing jokes and sometimes even doing deals. For example, they might let a rider come to the front for a moment of glory on his birthday, or as they enter his home town.

In the last section of the race all the riders in the peloton compete for the glory of finishing first. Sometimes a few cyclists will go to the front of the group and slow the pace, holding up the peloton while their team leader sprints ahead to take the lead.

The biggest danger in the peloton is crashing, because if one rider falls the others will either hit them or swerve to avoid the obstacle causing another collision.
Anything can cause a crash: a misjudgement by a rider, an over-enthusiastic fan standing in the way – even a dog wandering across the road.

Geraint Thomas

It can be fun in the peloton. We all know each other, as we race week in, week out together. A lot of the time my job will be to help the team sprinter or the guy trying to win the Tour de France. This is hard work as at various points you have to shelter them from the wind, keep them at the front and out of trouble, and get food or drinks. There's a great buzz if your teammate wins, and the whole team is happy when he goes on the podium.

Everyone knows the sprinter is the best and stands a chance of winning, but we ultimately know it's also a win for the team.

Just like in football, if a goal is scored it's the person who scored the goal that is publicly named, but the whole team has worked hard and helped to set them up for that goal.

In some races I have the team helping me. It helps to have done that job before so you really appreciate the work they do.

I don't like dropping out of the lead pack because I'm very competitive and it's a great challenge to try to be there in the real crunch parts of the race, when it really matters.

I'm the one in the black outfit, doing my bit to help the team in the peloton.

The climbs

The two main stages in the Tour de France are the mountain climbs, and the sprints on flatter terrain. On the flat stages of the Tour de France a good lead might be a few minutes – there is rarely a big gap between the leader and most of the pack. It is different in the mountains. A specialist sprinter will struggle up and down the peaks and could easily lose 30 minutes to his rivals over the day. The Tour de France can be won and lost in these climbs and descents – only the best riders can cope with them. Indeed, good sprinters who know they can't win the race overall sometimes withdraw from the race rather than face a tough day climbing and descending the peaks.

The first mountain ascent was introduced in 1905 when the route took in two peaks on the edge of the Alps between the towns of Grenoble and Gap. The 103-kilometre route took a horse-drawn stagecoach 12 hours. The first riders completed it in a third of that time, and carried on pedalling through the day. The public were impressed at their speed, strength and determination.

As the route changes every year, riders have to face different mountains. The most famous is L'Alpe d'Huez, where 300,000 fans have been known to line the steep course to watch riders climb a 13-kilometre stretch of zigzagging roads with an average **gradient** of 7.9%. The mountains are graded for their difficulty: four for the easiest to one for the most challenging steepness. L'Alpe d'Huez is grade one.

From 1933 the first riders to reach the top of a mountain peak have earned points to win the coveted title "King of the Mountains". Spaniard Vicente Trueba was the first. Since 1975 the winner of the mountain stages has worn a white jersey with red dots. The colours and pattern matched the packaging of its first sponsor, a chocolate maker, and haven't changed since.

Frenchman Richard Virenque won a record seven "King of the Mountains" titles in the Tour de France between 1994 and 2004. He said that he always looked straight ahead to see how his rivals were doing, what gears they were using and if their breathing was getting heavy. If he sensed they were weakening, he attacked. When he found himself struggling with the climb, the one place he didn't look was up, to see what was ahead of him.

Richard Virenque, 2004

What goes up must come down, and for the cyclists perhaps the most terrifying experience is hurtling down a mountain at up to 90 kilometres an hour on thin tyres, coping with the tight twists of the road. Streams or rainwater running across roads make bike brakes almost useless, and there is always the risk of a rider simply misjudging a bend and coming off. It is not unknown for riders to save themselves by jumping off bikes that are later found hanging from the branches of a tree over a steep drop.

Wartime hero

One famous climber used his cycling skills and fame in an unusual way. In 1938, Italy's Gino Bartali became the first man to win both the "King of the Mountains" and overall Tour de France titles. Bartali won the event again ten years later. Between those wins came the Second World War, during which Bartali carried messages on his bike for the Italian Resistance. He even built a trailer in which he hid Jewish people and carried them to safety. Bartali always wore a racing jersey with his name on, and because he was so famous the authorities did not dare to stop and check his bike and trailer.

Geraint Thomas

Climbs are really tough! In the UK we don't have many big mountains, like the Alps, so it's hard to train properly and I've always struggled going uphill as fast as some of the other riders. It's worse if you get left behind, which is known as being "dropped". On my first Tour I was dropped on a climb. For most of the day it was just me, a police motorbike and our second team car. It was hard. I got to the bottom of the first climb of the day and my arms felt like jelly and my legs fuzzy and I still had 70 kilometres to go and another three climbs. After about 40 kilometres of more climbing and some quite scary descents, I suddenly saw the gruppetto up ahead – that's a group of riders behind the lead peloton – I had caught them up! That felt like a real result.

cycling with Kim Kirchen during stage 10 of the 2007 Tour de France between Tallard and Marseille

The sprints

A sprint can be the most exciting sight of the Tour de France, as riders hurtle towards the finishing line at up to 70 kilometres an hour, pumping out a last burst of power. Many stages end in a sprint, and there are sometimes mini-sprints called "hot spots" during the middle of a stage as well.

Even the best sprinter needs help from the rest of his team though. Firstly, the team surrounds him during the stage, protecting him from the worst of the air drag and crosswinds. Secondly, they set the pace for him. This may be a really fast average time to tire out the legs of rivals, or a slower rate that saves energy if they are confident that their sprinter is the fastest over the last few metres. The later they leave that final push, the less time other competitors have to react.

The final kilometre of each stage is marked by a red triangle flag hung over the road. As a sprint stage nears its end, the team around its top sprinter peel off one by one, leaving the two or three fastest riders until last. Since Tour stages always finish in a town, sometimes sprinters have to pedal over cobbles rather than a smooth road, with even more chance of falling off.

Sprinting is high risk: everything happens so fast that there is little time to correct a mistake. The sprinters have a choice about whether to "hold their line", which means staying in the same part of the road, or moving across to block the path of other riders to stop them overtaking on that side. This is not popular with those riders behind and sometimes there are arguments between competitors about whether their riding was fair or safe.

First held on the Tour de France in 1934, the time trial is a race against the clock and interspersed throughout the race. There are both individual and team time-trial stages. In the individual trial, riders set off every two minutes, on their own, so that they cannot draft in the slipstream of a team-mate. This is why the time trial is sometimes called the "Race of Truth". Riders often switch to special streamlined bikes and wear **tapered** helmets to achieve the best **aerodynamic** shape. It's on time trials that you'll see the riders most consistently following the saying "stay low, go fast".

As well as earning points for winning sprint stages, riders also earn points from time trials and this can contribute to winning the sprinters' green jersey. This was introduced on the 50th anniversary of the race, in 1953, and is green because the first sponsor was a lawn-mower firm.

Sometimes, the Tour de France organisers include a team trial in the first week of the event. The results are decided by the finishing time of the fifth team member, to promote teamwork rather than individual success. But for the time-trial stages later in the Tour de France, the riders who leave last have the advantage of knowing the times their rivals achieved and so have a target to beat.

Speedy sprinter

Sprinters are bigger than other cyclists because they need to generate more power in short bursts. One of the biggest is the Spaniard Miguel Indurain, who between 1991 and 1995 became the first rider to win the Tour de France five times in a row. He achieved this by doing well in time trials and staying with the pack on the mountains where he was less comfortable. Tests showed that his lungs can hold an extra large amount of oxygen and he has an unusually strong heart. His build, combined with great determination and mental strength, has made him one of the best sprinters the Tour de France has known.

Geraint Thomas

I love sprints: I like the adrenaline buzz I get from jostling for position, trying to be at the front but not in the wind. My role in the sprint is usually to get our best sprinter at or near the front with 200 metres to go. For example, for a flat stage I'll be out at the front with the sprinter, and on a hilly day I'll stay back at the last climb to shade him from the wind, as I'm not as strong on the hill sections and need to save my energy as much as I can to allow me to keep going for the full three weeks. To know someone is relying on you is a big pressure!

The worst thing about a big bunch sprint is the danger of crashing. You don't see it coming, it just happens, though this is a bonus because there are few things worse than knowing you're about to smack into the ground at 60 kilometres an hour.

In my worst crash the guy in front of me hit a piece of metal in the road. It flipped up into my front wheel and stopped me dead. I fell forward and landed on my handlebars. I got a really bad injury that could have killed me.

I'd ruptured my spleen and they had to operate to take it out, because it wouldn't stop bleeding. It was so painful, and my stomach muscles were battered and bruised after the operation, but after only six weeks of recovery I was back on my bike again. I'm fortunate that there are really good doctors in British cycling, so I had a lot of support around me. Since then I've had quite a few falls and broken lots of bones.

When I fall off I usually curl up into a ball, making myself as small as possible to avoid getting whacked by 70 cyclists shooting past. I always wear a helmet and it has protected me from even worse injuries in all my crashes – I'd never dream of not wearing it. You don't think of the risks when you're cycling, though. You have to keep going or you'd stop racing.

The big finish

The last stage of the Tour finishes in Paris with several laps of the Avenue des Champs-Élysées, a famous street in the city centre. Excited crowds line the route and turn the day into a party.

The likely overall winner is usually known by this stage, because he'll have built up a lead over the previous three weeks.

But competitors, especially French riders, are eager for the glory of coming first in this dramatic setting. They suffer for it, too, because the Champs-Élysées has sections of cobbles that make for a very bumpy time in the saddle.

After the race the riders coast a final lap of the Champs-Élysées, celebrating the achievement of completing the Tour de France and knowing that there were more bikes at the starting point than have made it to Paris. Then the prizes are presented to the overall winner, the "King of the Mountains", the best sprinter and the fastest rider under the age of 26, plus the team prize.

For many years the prize money was the reason competitors raced. The first winner in 1903, Garin, used it to set himself up with a petrol station business. Today's cyclists are well paid by their sponsors, and the money is shared within the team in recognition of the fact that no individual can win this title on his own.

The three jerseys

Only one man has claimed all three jerseys at the end of a Tour de France, and, amazingly, he was competing for the first time. Eddie Merckx, of Belgium, won the overall title in 1969, gaining the yellow jersey, plus the prizes for best sprinter and climber. If the white jersey for best rider under 26 had existed, he would have won that too as he was only 24 years old. Merckx was nicknamed "The Cannibal" because he ate up the miles on the road, and chewed up his rivals by defeating them so easily.

One prize that is not awarded by the officials is the red lantern to the last finisher. The red lantern is named after a light that was once hung from the back of trains. Riders who realised they couldn't win first prize would compete for it because it gave them publicity, which meant they got paid more by sponsors. There are tales of competitors hiding in alleys, waiting for their rivals to pass them before rejoining the race. The organisers don't recognise the award, but the cycling world always knows who gets the red lantern.

The Tour de France is the greatest cycling race in the world and one of the toughest tests for any athlete. It enthralls millions of spectators every year, and every professional cyclist dreams of winning it.

Geraint Thomas

I had to work very hard just to complete my first Tour de France in 2007. Every day is so exhausting and every day is important, so after a week I was already starting to feel tired and finding the daily recovery more of a struggle. But I won the white jersey and felt really proud of that achievement.

In 2011 the race was still hard, but this time I was struggling at the front rather than at the back on my own – and I was able to win the white jersey again.

My endurance is getting better as I train more. It's a long three weeks on the road, going from hotel to hotel, so it's a great feeling to finish and see my family waiting for me at the finish line. When I see the Eiffel Tower on the last day it feels incredible.

with my Sky team-mates

The organisers are now changing the race slightly with the inclusion of the team time trials and shorter stages, which keeps the race fresh. My team is getting stronger and stronger, so hopefully we can win the race in the next year or so. I would love to try to win the whole race myself – hopefully it will happen one day. There's plenty of time, though. The Tour de France will be around for another 100 years, I'm sure!

Glossary

aerodynamic	the flow of air around an object
antiquity	the ancient past
consistent	repeatedly performing to the same standard
endurance	carrying on no matter how difficult the task
francs	French currency before the Euro
gradient	a slope
implementing	putting into action
insulated	kept hot or cold by the addition of a protective outer material
le maillot jaune	French for "the yellow jersey"
manual worker	someone who works with their hands
pantheon	a group of important people
publicity	attention given by television, radio or newspapers
revolutions	circular movements round a central point
rival	someone or something in fierce competition with the other
slipstream	an air gap created behind a moving vehicle
sprockets	points on the edge of a wheel that slot into the links of a chain
spokes	wire rods connecting the centre of a wheel to its outer edge
titles	championship races
velodrome	a cycle racing track with steeply curved sides

Index

What it takes to win a Tour de France jersey

Title	"King of the Mountains"	Best sprinter

What they win	white jersey with red dots	green jersey
Skills needed	• endurance • strength • ability to use tactics to beat rivals	• powerful leg muscles • excellent fitness for short bursts of speed • good concentration to avoid crashing in the pack

Best cyclist under 26	Overall winner

white jersey	yellow jersey
• endurance • strength • tactics	• consistency and endurance over 3 weeks • ability to cycle over all types of terrain • faster and stronger than other cyclists

Ideas for reading

Written by Clare Dowdall BA(Ed), MA(Ed)
Lecturer and Primary Literacy Consultant

Learning objectives: understand underlying themes, causes and points of view; sustain engagement with longer texts using different techniques to make the text come alive; use the techniques of dialogic talk to explore ideas, topics or issues; set own challenges to extend achievement and experience in writing

Curriculum links: Geography: Passport to the world; History: What can we learn about recent history from studying the life of a famous person?

Interest words: peloton, velodrome, le maillot jaune, masseurs, soigneurs, derailleur gears, sprocket, gradient, gruppetto

Resources: whiteboard, internet

Getting started

This book can be read over two or more reading sessions.

- Look at the front cover and read the blurb together. Ask children who has seen the Tour de France on television, or in real life. Share knowledge about the race and riders.

- Discuss what the terrain and climate are like in France in July, when the race is held. Establish that this is a gruelling race conducted in tough conditions.

- Using the glossary, help children to read, pronounce and understand interest words, e.g. peloton.

Reading and responding

- Ask children to read to p16, noting the language and structural features of this book, e.g. facts written in the present tense, historical information recounted in the past tense.

- Focus on p9. Ask children to explain why Desgrange wrote as if the riders were superheroes, and what he was trying to achieve.

- Ask children to read to the end of the book, looking for the different locations that are mentioned and making notes on how the race changed over the years.